Animal Skins

by Mary Holland

Fur (hair), feathers and scales are animal skin coverings that look very different from each other but do many of the same things. They can keep an animal warm and dry, protect an animal from predators, warn other animals to stay away, or even help an animal hide (camouflage).

The wings and bodies of moths and butterflies are covered with tiny, powdery scales.

The scales on this moth's wings are colored to look like big eyes to scare off predators.

cicada skin

Our skin grows with us, but an insect's skin (exoskeleton) does not grow. Like snakes, when a young insect's skin gets too tight, it must replace it. The insect makes a new, larger skin under its old one and then sheds its old skin. Some insects shed their skin many times before they become an adult.

After a young cicada grows wings, it splits its skin one final time and flies away.

Porcupines are mammals, and like all mammals, they have hair. Porcupines have three kinds of hair:

- Underfur – short and thick, keeps the porcupine warm in winter
- Guard hairs – long, sensitive hairs, act like whiskers, letting a porcupine know when it brushes against something
- Quills – stiff, pointed hair used for protection

Quills are hard, hollow, and pointed, with little hooks at their tips. If you touch one, it will stick into you. But don't worry — if you don't touch a porcupine, you won't get any quills in you. A porcupine cannot throw its quills any more than you can throw your hair!

A striped skunk is a mammal and has a black-and-white coat of hair. If an animal really bothers it, a skunk can spray it with a smelly liquid that comes out under its tail. Most animals don't get near skunks because they know that its striped coat means "stay away or I'll spray you!"

Young deer, or fawns, have no way of defending themselves if a predator comes along. To keep from being discovered, fawns have no scent for the first few days after they are born. During their first summer they are also covered with white spots. These spots help them blend in to the woods and fields where they live, so they won't be noticed.

Instead of hairs, birds have feathers. Feathers do lots of things—help a bird fly, attract a mate and keep warm. When a bird gets cold, it can puff out its feathers and make little pockets of warm air in between them, next to its skin. These pockets of air help keep this blue jay warm even when it is snowing.

female

Sometimes the color of an animal's skin covering can tell you whether you are looking at a male or a female animal. Many male birds have more brightly colored feathers than females. Can you think why this might be? The female bird usually sits on the nest and incubates the eggs. Would bright feathers be easier to see? Why would a bird on a nest full of eggs or nestlings not want to be seen?

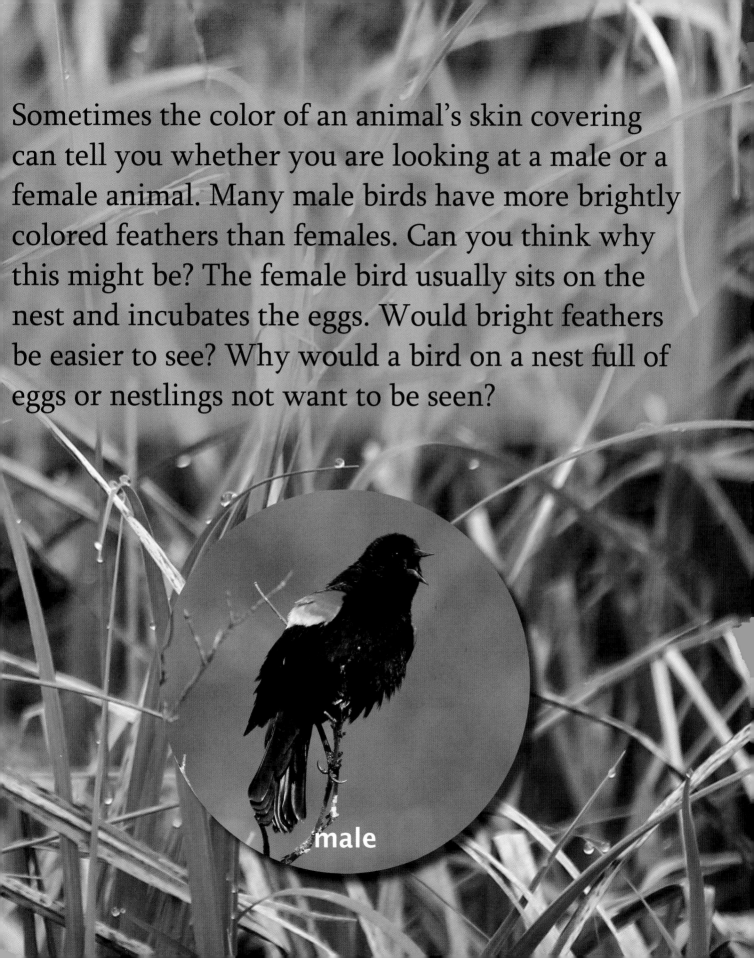

male

Frogs can do something with their skin that you and I can't–they can breathe through it! Frogs have lungs and take in air through their noses, like we do, but they also absorb oxygen through their skin. When they are under water or buried in soil, frogs only breathe through their skin, not their lungs. In order for them to do this, their skin must remain moist.

Like snakes, frogs regularly shed their old skin. However, unlike snakes, they pull it off over their head with their front feet and then they eat it!

Sometimes the color of an animal's skin can save its life! Red efts are salamanders that live on land. Many animals would get very sick if they ate a red eft. The color red can mean danger. When salamander-eating predators see the red eft's red skin, they know not to eat it!

The American toad's skin is also poisonous to some animals. It isn't colored brightly like the red eft's skin, but there are bumps all over it. Inside these bumps there is a liquid that tastes bad and will make some animals sick if they eat it. However, holding an American toad is not dangerous—you will not get sick or get warts!

Snakes are not slimy! They are reptiles, and, like all reptiles, have thick sections of dry skin called scales. Some snakes have smooth scales, some have rough. Scales are hard and protect a snake from predators. They also help a snake move.

A snake never stops growing. The more it eats the faster it grows. A snake's skin cannot grow, so when it gets too tight, a snake grows a new, bigger skin and sheds the old one. If you look closely at a shed snake skin you can see the scales.

Snakes don't have eyelids. Instead, they have special see-through scales (spectacles) that cover and protect their eyes. Can you find them?

Like snakes, turtles are reptiles. In addition to having scales on its head, legs and tail, a turtle also has special scales on its shell, called scutes. They form a kind of skin over the bony shell. The scutes are made out of the same material (keratin) as the horns, beaks and nails of other animals.

Different animals have different types of skin covering and use it in different ways. Do you have fur (hair), feathers or scales? How does your skin covering help you?

For Creative Minds

Match the Skin to the Animal

Match each animal to its skin.

A — spotted salamander

B — porcupine

C — European starling

D — snapping turtle

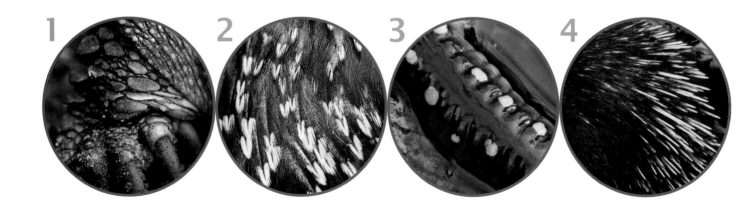

1   2   3   4

Answers: A3, B4, C2, D1

How Animals Use Their Skins

Which of these animals uses its skin to:

1. breathe	2. crawl	3. keep warm
4. defend itself	5. camouflage itself	6. warn others

Some animals may use their skin for more than one purpose.

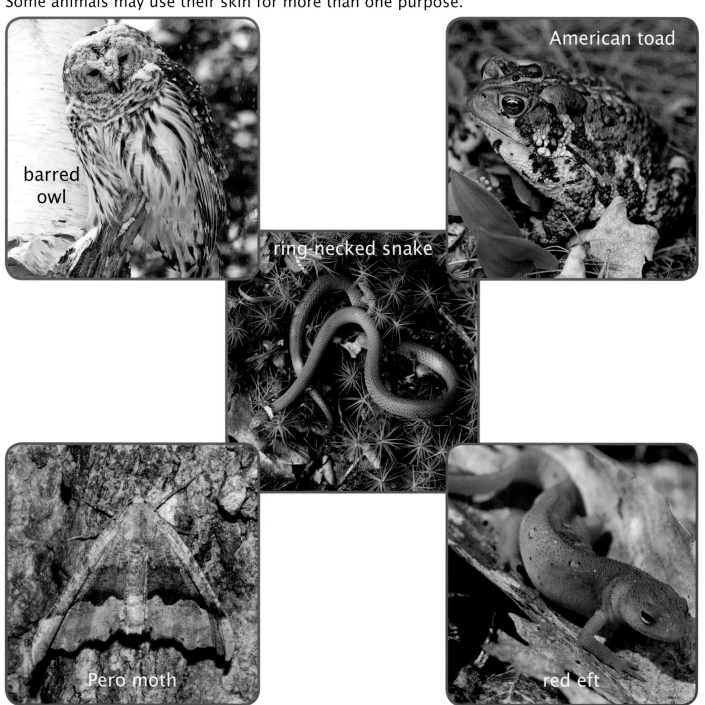

Answers: to breathe: American toad, red eft; to crawl along the ground: ring-necked snake; to keep warm: barred owl; to defend itself: American toad; to camouflage itself : Pero moth, American toad, barred owl; to warn others: red eft

Special Skins

Hairy-tailed Mole: Moles spend most of their life underground, in tunnels that they dig with their front feet. The fur coat of moles is short, soft and velvety. It can easily move forward or backward, so that the mole can travel in tight tunnels without getting stuck.

European Honey Bee: Honey bees are covered with branched hairs. As they travel from flower to flower collecting pollen grains for food for their hive, some of the pollen gets caught in their hairs. When honey bees visit a flower, some of the pollen covering their body is left behind and helps turn flowers into fruits (pollination).

Turkey Vulture: While most of a turkey vulture is covered with feathers, its red head is almost featherless. The reason for this may be so that when this scavenger is eating a decaying animal, it does not soil head feathers when it reaches into the rotting carcass to feed. The lack of feathers on its head may also help it stay cool in the summer, as heat from its body can escape more easily if it's not trapped by feathers.

Gray Treefrog: Gray treefrogs have the ability to change the color of their skin. They can be gray, green or brown, depending on the temperature, amount of light and their surroundings. Gray treefrogs tend to become darker when it is cold or dark, and lighter when it is hot and sunny. Their mottled skin blends in with bark, making it very hard to find them when they are on a branch.

Skins and Animal Classes

Animals with backbones are divided into five different groups, or classes: fish, birds, reptiles, mammals and amphibians. One of the several ways that scientists sort animals into these classes is by their skin covering!

- Mammals have fur (hair) at some point in their lives.
- Fish have moist scales.
- Birds are the only animals that have feathers.
- Amphibians have smooth, wet skin.
- Reptiles have dry scales.

Looking at their skin coverings, can you identify to which animal class these animals belong?

bear   owl   frog

snake   human   fish

Answers: Mammals: bear, human; Fish: fish; Bird: owl; Amphibian: frog; Reptile: snake

To Lily Piper, whose skin is so very soft—MH

Thanks to Sarah Chatwood, Master Naturalist and Educator with Montana Audubon for verifying the accuracy of the information in this book.

Thanks to Erin Donahue for the photo of Otis Brown used in the book.

Library of Congress Cataloging-in-Publication Data

Names: Holland, Mary, 1946- author.
Title: Animal skins / by Mary Holland.
Description: Mt. Pleasant, SC : Arbordale Publishing, [2019] | Series: Animal anatomy and adaptations | Audience: Ages 4-9. | Audience: K to grade 3. | Includes bibliographical references.
Identifiers: LCCN 2018050175 (print) | LCCN 2018053186 (ebook) | ISBN 9781643513423 (Pdf) | ISBN 9781643513447 (ePub 3) | ISBN 9781643513461 (Read aloud interactive) | ISBN 9781643513393 (hardcover) | ISBN 9781643513409 (pbk.) | ISBN 9781643513416 (spanish pbk.)
Subjects: LCSH: Body covering (Anatomy)--Juvenile literature. | Skin--Juvenile literature. | Adaptation (Biology)--Juvenile literature.
Classification: LCC QL941 (ebook) | LCC QL941 .H65 2019 (print) | DDC 591.47--dc23
LC record available at https://lccn.loc.gov/2018050175

Lexile® Level: 640
key phrases: animal adaptations
Animals in this book include wood frog (cover), American bittern (title page); blinded sphinx moth, cicada, porcupine, striped skunk, white-tailed deer fawn, blue jay, male and female red-winged blackbirds, green frog, red eft, American toad, common garter snake, and human (Otis Brown)

Bibliography/ Bibliografía:
Halfmann, Janet. Fur and Feathers. Mt. Pleasant, SC: Arbordale Publishing, 2010. Book.
Holland, Mary. *Naturally Curious: A Photographic Field Guide and Month-By-Month Journey Through the Fields, Woods, and Marshes of New England*. North Pomfret, VT: Trafalgar Square Books, 2010. Book.

Printed in China, May 2019
This product conforms to CPSIA 2008
First Printing

Arbordale Publishing
Mt. Pleasant, SC 29464
www.ArbordalePublishing.com